Ancient Stones

The Prehistoric Dolmens of Sicily

ANCIENT STONES

The Prehistoric Dolmens of Sicily

Salvatore Piccolo

Introduction by Timothy Darvill OBE

Brazen Head Publishing

Brazen Head Publishing
Lombardy House, Thornham, Norfolk, PE36 6LX, United Kingdom

www.brazenheadpublishing.co.uk

Published in the United Kingdom
by Brazen Head Publishing 2013

First published in Italy in 2007 by Morrone Editore as 'Antiche Pietre. La Cultura dei Dolmen nella Preistoria della Sicilia Sud-Orientale'

Copyright © Salvatore Piccolo 2013

Translation copyright © Jean Woodhouse 2013

Preface copyright © Timothy Darvill 2013

All images are copyright © of the author unless otherwise stated.

All rights reserved. No part of this publication may be reproduced, stored in a retrieval system, transmitted in any form or by any means, without the prior permission in writing of Brazen Head Publishing. Within the UK, exceptions are allowed in respect of any fair dealing for the purpose of research or private study, or criticism or review, as permitted under the Copyright, Design and Patents Act, 1988, or in the case of reprographic reproduction in accordance with the terms of licenses issued by the Copyright Licensing Agency. Enquiries concerning reproduction outside those terms in other countries should be sent to the Rights Department, Brazen Head Publishing, at the address above. This book is sold subject to the conditions that it shall not, by way of trade or otherwise, be lent, re-sold, hired out, or otherwise circulated without the publisher's prior consent in any form of binding or cover other than that in which it is published and without a similar condition including this condition being imposed on the subsequent purchaser.

International Standard Book Number (ISBN): 978-0-9565106-2-4

*For my wife Gina and
my sons Silvio, Cristina and Lucrezia*

CONTENTS

Acknowledgements | ix

Introduction | xi

1. THE QUESTION OF ORIGINS | 1
2. COMPARISON OF FOUR DOLMENS | 9
3. UMBILICUS MUNDI | 31

Chronology of Sicilian Prehistory | 37

Bibliography | 39

Index | 45

Acknowledgements

I wish to thank all those who offered information and material, *in primis* Ferdinando Lazzarini who, with outstanding technical ability, produced the drawings of the Avola and Cava dei Servi dolmens; Dr Giuseppe Cassataro, for having guided me to the site of the Monte Bubbonia dolmen which would have otherwise been difficult to locate; Antonio Catalano, for the drawings he did at the Monte Bubbonia monument; my wife, Gina Pardo, for the topographical analysis of the "Cava Lazzaro"; Dr Gaetano Ciancio, son of Salvatore Ciancio who discovered the Avola "dolmen", for having given me access to his father's library; Dr Pietro Calabrese, Home Office, for having allowed me to take part in his studies on "Indo-European populations" which, unfortunately, have not yet been published; my friend Dr Giuseppe Ansaldi who, in the name of real friendship, carried out the geological analysis on the pseudo dolmen of Avola.

A special thanks goes to Professor Sebastiano Tusa, my old lecturer of Paleethnology at the University School for technical scientific specialists of the Italian Archaeological Heritage, for following my initial research and his own inspirational important work on the megalithic phenomena in Sicily.

Salvatore Piccolo

Introduction

Megalithic monuments unfailingly excite attention. Not only are they impressive structures in the modern landscape, but they also provide that thread of continuity from prehistoric times to the present day that allows us to explore our history and our humanity. Such monuments have long been recognized across Europe from the shores of the Mediterranean to the Baltic, from the Atlantic to the Black Sea coasts. They have intrigued scholars for centuries and with the scientific and technical advances of modern archaeology we are finally beginning to understand something of their purpose and the meanings they had to those who built them. Those same researches are also revealing the chronology of the sites, emphasizing the numerous different traditions across time and space. Many of these monuments turn out to be fairly short-lived, the focus of ceremonies and celebrations for just a few generations.

The megaliths of the central Mediterranean are not well-known compared to those in other parts of Europe, nor are they known-well in terms of their date and cultural associations. In this book Salvatore Piccolo introduces a group of sites in Sicily that usefully expands the horizons of the megalithic world. The sites discussed illustrate the range and scale of the monumental architecture involved and, one might hope, will lead to the discovery of further examples to enrich and extend their distribution across the island. The discovery of early Bronze Age Castelluccian pottery at Cava dei Servi provides the first real clues as to the date and cultural context of these sites. It is a discovery that adds support to the idea of connections between Sicily and Malta at this time. The dozen or so Maltese dolmens are certainly alike in form and scale, and are widely seen as post-temple period constructions. Both groups may also be connected with the cluster of dolmens forming the Otranto group at the extreme southern tip of the 'Heel' of Italy.

Ancient Stones will no doubt provide the inspiration for further research. Having identified the first crop of sites and described them in detail, much now needs to be done to explore them, understand them, and also to conserve them and present them to the local visitors and tourists alike. Here though we begin the task of bringing the dolmen culture of Sicily back to life.

Timothy Darvill OBE
Professor of Archaeology, Bournemouth University, UK

1 The Question of Origins

First studies

Megalithic architecture, or the construction of sanctuaries, tombs, and other edifaces, using enormous blocks of stone, occupies an important position in the cultural experience of Neolithic Europe.

The word *dolmen*, which derives from the Breton word '*taol*' meaning table and '*maen*' meaning stone, appears in the scientific literature around the end of the 1700's. Until that time the examination of these "strange" monuments scattered here and there gave way to suppositions that were, to say the least, fanciful. It was thought they were built by giants or, indeed, deeds of the devil. The first explorations were therefore to understand the use of these structures and establish their age, even though the absence of metal objects indicated the period they appertained to.

In the second half of the 1800's, the publication of the first map of known megalithic localities highlighted so many coincidences this led to the belief that they were the work of one unique *population*. Thus it seemed justifiable to consider the "megalithic phenomena" an unusual cultural manifestation of the Middle East and *dolmens*, in definition, the unnatural reproduction of the Mediterranean burial grotto[1].

The Australian archaeologist *Vere Gordon Childe* reinforced this hypothesis in his final book. He claimed that the construction of the enormous mausoleums was carried out by mythical *megalithic missionaries*, members of some early Aegean tribes, of the eastern Mediterranean, who divulged a religious faith belonging to the cults of Gaea the Mother Goddess, goddess of the earth[2].

The perfection of absolute dating systems, thanks to the 14C method, put an end to this hypothesis once and for all. It was proven that the oldest megalithic tombs originated in central Europe. Breton dolmens date back to 4500 BC (earlier than the Egyptian pyramids, Mesopotamian ziggurats[3] and the great Cretan and Mycenae sites). They spread further south to central and southern France, southwest to Spain and Portugal and north-east to the central lowlands of Europe, Sweden and elsewhere[4]. Concluding their phase with the most recent constructions in Malta, around 2400 BC and in Italy at the beginning of the second millennium BC.

The above time range was sufficient for each region to evolve a local typology though keeping a common characteristic: the use of blocks or slabs of stone, at

Vere Gordon Childe
(1892–1957)

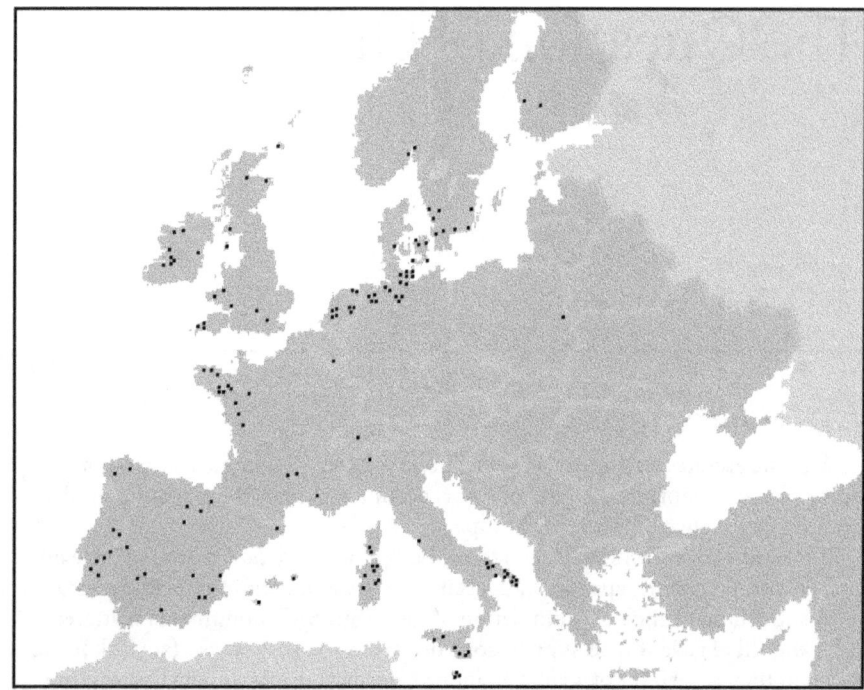

Map indicating the diffusion of Megalithic monuments throughout Europe

times colossal in dimension, which made them a phenomena tied to a relatively widespread culture.

Principal characteristics of dolmens

The most elementary configuration of the dolmen is trilithic: a horizontal slab of stone placed on top of two vertically positioned stones in order to form a construction where the structural elements frame a quadrangular space. More complex forms made up of a long succession of triliths followed, thereby generating two particular forms: the *corridor tomb* and the *gallery tomb* (allée couverte)[5]. The *corridor tombs*, made of big slabs of stone vertically fixed into the ground, *orthostats*, have corridors that vary in length and lead to a *Dolmen* chamber or a number of chambers of a polygonal shape[6]. The *gallery tombs*, instead, have just one rectangular-shaped space wholly reserved as a sepulchral chamber.

Some of these evolved into rather complicated constructions, as in the case of the *false dome* dolmens where the convex roof was obtained by gradually decreasing the distance between the slabs of the building[7]. Another instance is that of the dolmens *with lateral chambers*; characterised by a series of cells around the central one. Each sepulchre, or series of sepulchres, was completed by being covered with earth mixed with stones[8].

Not all were funeral monuments: the cromlechs[9] of Stonehenge in England

A.
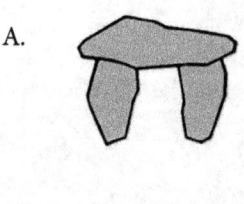
B.
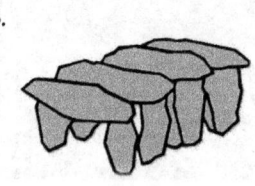

A. Dolmen, B. Allée Couverte

The Carnac menhirs (Brittany)

and the Carnac menhirs[10] in France, to mention some, would have served other extraordinary purposes, perhaps connected to the practice of an astronomical cult. Without any doubt, they represent the product of a Culture that captured the irradiation centre of absolute positive energy in the Universe.

Inestimable problems had to be faced in whichever region they were, whether concerning finding suitable stones or transporting the material for construction. In those areas where the stone was extremely hard and difficult to shatter they raised enormous monuments[11]; whereas in other places where the stone was easy to chip, dry-stone method structures were built rather than using the real megalithic technique. The latter is the case of the island od Sicily.

The "prototype" of this architecture certainly had its origins in a series of lucky coincidental factors. The surprise that was stirred up by some natural trilithic "scenery" must have let loose the religious imagination of certain prehistoric communities. So much so, an exceptional mystic significance was given to the stone triads.

Mediterranean dolmens

As already mentioned, Mediterranean dolmens date back to an era closer to ours. Around a hundred can be found throughout Sardinia, some of which, the so-called *dolmen cysts*[12] made up of stone slabs assembled in cubiform manner, are dated back to the Copper Age, around 3000–2100 BC. This model of construction is also found in Sicily, in Butera in the province of Caltanissetta to be precise. It is in the new area of *Piano della fiera* where a prehistoric necropolis still stands. Used again in the Greek period, the monument takes us back to mixed cult practices, both Hellenic and indigenous, and characterised by the positioning of human remains inside urns, *enchytrismós,* which in turn, were placed inside these small chambers[13]. Dolmens in Apulia, which are more recent, date back to the first half of the second millennium BC, the period corresponding to the ancient phase of the *Bronze Age*[14].

The typology of these is varied: ranging from gallery dolmens in the hinterland

Dolmen cyst of Butera, Caltanissetta

The Megalithic complex of Stonehenge, England

of Bari and Taranto, to the small rectangular or polygonal structures in the Salento region and, hence, to the *small specchie*[15] containing one or more dolmen chamber monuments. Most of the dolmens of this region have favoured the hypothesis of having come from across the sea, as they are situated along the coast.

To the south, the islands of Malta and Gozo are home to the most extraordinary prehistoric sites of the Mediterranean, the "megalithic temples". They were built between about 4000 and 2500 BC[16]. They were dedicated to a cult worshipping a fertility goddess. The dolmens, as they should be correctly called, (around twenty in all) are to be dated back to a successive period (the second half of the third millennium BC). In most cases we are dealing with small chambers here, with the cover made of a large slab placed on upright stones. They are claimed to belong to a population certainly different from that which built the previous megalithic temples. It is presumed the population arrived from the Salento peninsular because of the similarity to the constructions found in Malta and Apulia[17].

In recent years the presence of these man-made tombs and their purpose are also being revealed in Sicily. Small dolmen monuments are being found almost everywhere, both inland and along the coast of our region[18]. Many of them are only memories of the people of the area, having been destroyed by uncontrolled speculation of the land. I found this out for myself. Probably, others are there still hidden under heaps of earth waiting to reveal the secret of their origin.

Notes

1. Pigorini, L. (1903) *Bullettino di Paletnologia Italiana*, **XXIX**, 199; Müller, S. (1907) *L'Europe Prehistorique*, Paris; Gervasio, M. (1913) *I dolmen e la civiltà del bronzo nella Puglie*, p. 317, Bari.
2. Childe, V.G. (1965) *Preistoria della Società Europea*, pp. 175 onwards.

3 *Ziggurats* were very high towers having the form of a terraced-step pyramid of successively receding stories, or levels, and topped with a small temple.
4 Fleming, A. (1972) *Recent advances in megalithic studies,* Origini **VI**, 301-307, Rome.
5 Until not many years ago, it was thought that this typology was of a Danish population, 3000 BC, which had been inspired by middle-eastern influxes. New data, however, indicate that the innovation came from people resident in Brittany, the north-west of France, back in 4000 BC.
6 This type of dolmen evolved in southern Spain around the fifth millennium BC. Indeed, tombs with corridors as long as thirty metres are present in this region.
7 We can find a dolmen where the *false dome* ceiling reaches six metres in height near *Newgrange,* County Meath, Eire.
8 The necessity to cover the structure with earth and stones was to render the original chamber more stable thus better built. The mound, or barrow, therefore, is seen as a protective element and indicative of underground monuments, some taking on colossal proportions. We can consider *Le Mont Saint Michel*, Morbihan, Normandy, measuring 115 x 58 m; *Newgrange*, near the city of Drogheda, Eire, is an immense circular dune, 115 m in diameter.
9 *Cromlechs* are megalithic monuments of enormous stones, set in a circle in the ground and capped with long blocks of stone like lintels.
10 The *menhir* is a megalithic monument of only one block of stone fixed vertically into the ground. In the case in question we allude to the famous *alignments* of the Carnac village on the southern coast of Brittany. There are three groups: the Menéc *alignment*, made up of 1,099 menhirs in 11 rows; Kermario, 1,029 menhirs in 10 rows; Kerlescan, 594 menhirs lined up in 13 rows and 39 pietrefitte (embedded stones) set in a semi-circle.
11 The English academic *Richard Atkinson,* who sustained the possibility of applying the experimental principle even to archaeological sciences, showed that seven hundred men fitted with robust leather ropes can lift a block of stone of almost forty tons. Eight men are able to move a mass of five hundred kilograms.

The Temple of Tarxien, Malta

Photography by Günther Hölbl, 1983; reproduced with permission.

[12] Puglisi, S.M. (1941-42) *Villaggi sotto roccia e sepolcri megalitici della Gallura*, Bullettino di Paletnologia Italiana, n.s., **5**, 123.

[13] Orlandini, P. (1962) *Kokalos* **VIII**, 79; Adamesteanu D., (1958) *Piano della fiera. Scavo nella necropoli,* Monumenti Antichi dell'Accademia dei Lincei, vol. **XLIV**, Rome.

[14] The radiometric data evaluations carried out on some organic remains found in the *La Muculufa* and *Monte Grande* settlements, both in the province of Agrigento, take us back to the end of the third millennium BC (about 2169 BC) the most ancient datings of the Sicilian Bronze Age; cf. Castellana, G. (2002) *La Sicilia nel II millennio a.C.,* pp. 12 onwards, Caltanissetta.

[15] *Specchie* are made up of an amalgam of different shaped stones and mud. They were erected for funeral purposes (*small specchie*) or for defence (*big specchie*).

[16] Bonanno, A. (2000) *Malta. Il fascino dell'archeologia,* p. 5, Malta.

[17] Evans, J.D. (1961) *Segreti dell'antica Malta,* pp.178-179, Milan.

[18] Guzzardi, L. (1996) *L'area degli Iblei fra l'età del bronzo e la prima età del ferro,* in: Civiltà indigene e città greche nella regione iblea, a cura di Lorenzo Guzzardi, Assessorato BB.CC.AA. della Regione Siciliana e Distretto scolastico 52, p.13, Ragusa; cf. also Tusa, S. (1997) *Il Megalitismo e la Sicilia,* in: Prima Sicilia. Alle origini della Società siciliana, a cura di Sebastiano Tusa, Regione Siciliana, Assessorato dei beni Culturali, Ambientali e della Pubblica Istruzione, pp. 333-341, Palermo.

2 Comparison of Four Dolmens

Monte Bubbonia

The Sicilian dolmen phenomenon has started to arouse interest among scholars, so much so that many reports, initially given little attention, are being reconsidered in the light of a new *forma mentis*.

The richest source of documentation seems to be accredited to the south-east, while the west, as known to date, has presumably only two megalithic constructions: the first in Sciacca, in the district of San Giorgio, the *femmina morta* site, and the other in the archaeological area of Mura Pregne, north-east of Monte San Mauro between Termini Imerese and Sciara[1].

We shall limit ourselves to the subtitle of this text, beginning with *Monte Bubbonia*, a majestic hill 595 metres high to the north of the city of Gela.

Travelling from Gela to Catania, taking the road *SS. 117*, follow the directions to Piazza Armerina; nine kilometres on there is a cross-roads and to the left the old road to Mazzarino. The road sign shows *Itinerarium Antoninii,* an old road map

The Mura Pregne dolmen (Palermo)

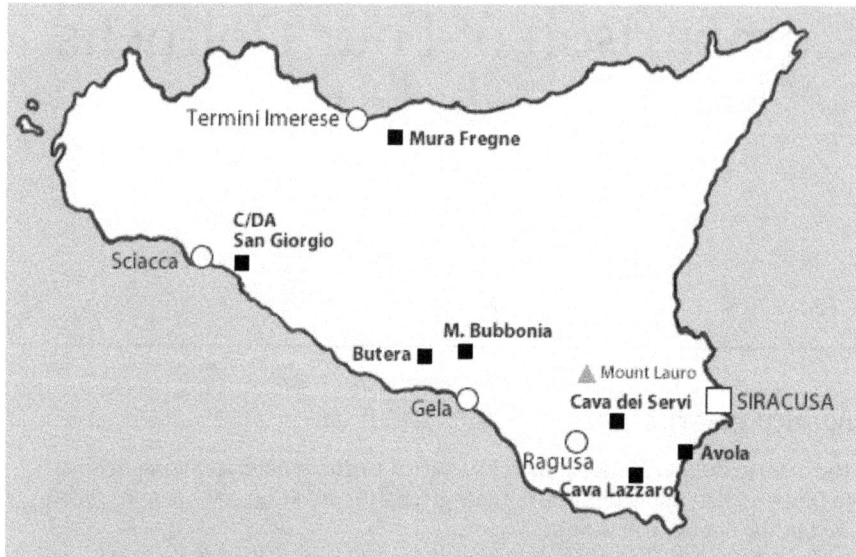

The locations of Sicilian dolmens (marked with a filled square)

from the time of the Roman Empire, documented importance of which is pointed out on an opportune tourist chart. The entrance to the mount is just three kilometres further on.

The geological conformation of the hill is quite recent, except for the lower chalk strata formed in the Miocene Age, 23 million to 5 million years ago. Around 700,000 years ago, the lower Pleistocene Age, it was covered by sea silt, quartz sand, quartzarenite and, lastly, by a thin layer of red sand that makes the location rather crumbly and dusty.

At the beginning of the 1900's, *Paolo Orsi,* led the first excavations[2]. He found an indigenous centre on the summit which had been colonised by Gela in the sixth century BC. *Piero Orlandini* recognised this as the ancient Sican city of *Maktorion* mentioned by Herodotus, the Greek historian par excellence[3]. *Paolo Orsi* was the first to identify the *dolmen* we are about to deal with[4], *Cassataro*[5] recorded it as did *Pancucci*[6] successively.

The monument is to be found some three quarters of the way along a track which runs along the eastern side of the hill and goes up towards the acropolis. It is in a position that notably overhangs an area of flat land that is surrounded by hills. Made of colossal splinters of rock, with no significant modifications, the *dolmen* is rectangular in shape. The chalk slab which acts as the cover, the back being wedged into the natural slope of the ground, rests on two parallel megaliths forming a chamber of about 2.60 m². The upright block on the right was shorter from the beginning and was raised with overlapping makeshift quoins, or wedges. The pits formed by the rudimentary wedges were filled with small stones.

The back wall was created by fitting together two polygon-shaped slabs. The slab on the right still today overlaps the cover, evidently protecting it from landslides; the other polygon slab, which was lower, had small irregular-shaped stones added to it. Frequent landslides have resulted in a visible tilting to the right,

Paolo Orsi (1859-1935)

causing a narrowing of the initial part of the chamber. The entrance, opening north-east, follows the same orientation of the other Sicilian dolmens.

A little lower down, following the natural inclination of the hillside, lies what was probably the closure slab. The dimensions, which correspond quite well to the main structure, indicate it could really be the closure hatch as it matches the two uprights.

The original architectural idea was without doubt a small *chamber tomb,* also to be found in Sardinia and in Apulia, with the back wall placed against the curve of the hillside to facilitate burial, as was the custom for this type of architecture. Soil and stony overlays are to be seen wherever these are found.

Even though the hill had undergone exhaustive works of reforestation, which will have deprived us of many clues, we do not hasten to connect the monument in question to the already examined prehistoric settlements on this north-eastern side of the hill. The latter date from the early *Bronze Age* to that of *Pantalica III and IV,* around 850–700 BC.[7]

At the time of the exploration, *Paolo Orsi* came across an elegant *boccaletto* (a small tankard) with faint traces of decoration[8], leading him to date the sepulchre back to the seventh century BC. We must not however forget that in the past, especially among people of less affluent classes, it was normal to use previously utilised objects. Hence, finding chronologically previous objects inside our artefact we must not be led astray. Instead, they will be defined in the light of further Sicilian dolmen research and study. It must be mentioned that Paolo Orsi, born in Rovereto, Trentino, had already collected signs in megalithic slabs he found in 1898 at Monte Racello, near the town of Comiso, Ragusa.

The Sciacca dolmen (Agrigento)

Technical data sheet of the monument

Overall length of the monument	2.20 m
Overall width of the monument	1.20 m
Length of the right lateral	1.25 m
Length of left lateral	2.10 m
Tilt of right lateral	20° to the left
Width of right slab (back wall)	0.78 m
Height of right slab (back wall)	1.00 m
Width of left slab (back wall)	0.60 m
Height of left slab (back wall)	0.52 m
Thickness of chalk mass	0.35 m
Length of closure hatch	1.30 m
Width of closure hatch	0.69 m
Thickness of closure slab	0.40 m
Height of monument	1.40 m
Orientation (opening)	24° NE

Geographical map references I.G.M. (Italian Military Geographic Institute)
1/25.000 -F° 272 I NE

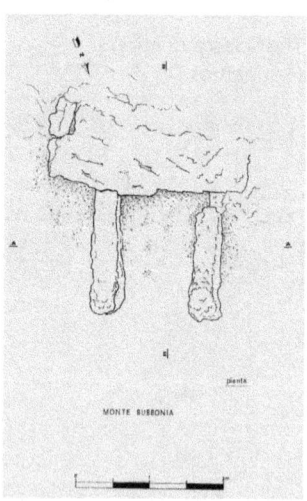

Monte Bubbonia dolmen
(ground plan)

The Monte Bubbonia dolmen (Caltanissetta)

Cava dei Servi

The River Tellesimo finds its source in the Iblean Plateau; its confluence with the River Tellaro is a few kilometres downstream. The Tellaro, by now swollen due to a number of other forks, flows into the Ionian Sea, south of Lido di Noto. There where the Tellesimo has its source, a tortuous path winding along through the jagged coastal range leads us to one of the many quarries called *Cava dei Servi*.

The place, some kilometres south of the hamlet of San Giacomo, opens onto a Nature Reserve which contains the most exceptional (an understatement) prehistoric finds.

The geological conformation of this area is rather varied, comprising an alternation of biocalcarenite (Lecce stone) cemented to grey-white macro-foraminiferous rock, in irregular banks from 50 cm to 2–3 m in thickness, and cream-white marnous calcarenite (limestone) which are thinly consolidated. They form the *Irminio Member* of the *Ragusa* formation; the upper member, the structure being in two parts, is divided (the lower part, the *Leonardo Member*, does not come to the surface in the area).

The clayey marnous terrain, highly erosive, is modelled into gently undulating sub-surface flatland giving origin to low hills which formed between the Upper Oligocene Age and the Lower Miocene Age (between twenty-six and twenty million years ago).

The erosive action of water determined very steep and deep ravines that characterise most of the territory around Ragusa and Syracuse, so giving a reason for the existence of inaccessible and aspen caves which have from time unknown given refuge to groups of humans.

In *Cava dei Servi*, the depression that has been formed by the torrents has made it impossible to reach a small headland, where a prehistoric acropolis probably once stood. The promontory is surrounded by steep rock faces that were connected to the mountain by a narrow and well-defined passage.

The hump was the site of human settlements from the early *Bronze Age* to the *Pantalica 1* period (around 1270–1000 BC)[9]; the era to which the innumerable *small artificial grotto* sepulchres that are hollowed out in the side of the rock faces belong[10]. There are, moreover, documented *enchytrismós* burials (inside large urns) and ceramic objects which will have made up the funeral dowry of the dead[11]. This area, which is not far from the Mount Lauro embankment, gave rise to interest as far back as the Copper Age because, as in the Iblean region, it guaranteed excellent commercial opportunities thanks to the quarrying of flint. Flint was easy to transport downhill along the waterways of the Tellaro and Anapo Rivers[12].

A medium-sized slab construction dominates a landscape that cannot but arouse mystic sensations. It is to be found on top of an overhanging rock, along one of the less tortuous paths of the quarry, few metres higher than the only track that leads to the gorge.

The semi-oval monument is formed by four rectangular slabs fixed into the ground. Another three slabs are on top, leaning in such a way they reduce the surface and form a *false dome*. Two large parallelepiped boulders complete the construction.

The Cava dei Servi dolmen (Ragusa)

The four upright stones that determine the curve are more or less uniform in measurement, which proves building abilities aimed at creating corresponding bonding of each construction element of the manufactured product. Hence, stability is guaranteed. The three inclining slabs that were placed on top instead have more irregular dimensions, having no stabilising function their precision would have been superfluous.

Inside the chamber there is a large chalky slab that has been fractured in four places. It would seem it was the vault stone of the monument and that it crashed to the ground due to progressive sliding of the structure. Along with some findings underneath, which we shall discuss further on, its dimensions seem to consolidate the *coffer* theory. All the pieces on the ground, in fact, would have been part of a large monolith, squared in front to fit the closure hatch. The blocks to the side served as jams, reinforcing a part that was rather under pressure because of frequent opening. The lay-out of the stones gave shape to a construction of about 3.00 m^2 that had been set into the slope of the hill to make burial easier.

A lucky chance, to say the least, led me to determine the function and chronology of this unique piece of work; thanks to numerous human bone fragments[13] (the only organic clues so far found inside a Mediterranean dolmen) and to some splinters of Castelluccian (Early Bronze Age) ceramics[14]. The anthropological remains have confirmed the burial purpose of the artefact, while the, though few, earthenware fragments have legitimised dating them back to the early *Bronze Age*.

The positioning around a rocky cemetery confirms the belief that we are not dealing with an attempt to better a particularly demanding and dangerous architectural structure, like the *small artificial grotto*[15], but we are faced with absolutely unique *elaborations*.

The location, therefore, will have also had a dolmen necropolis. This is not such

Anthropological remains found by the author in the Cava dei Servi dolmen and, in the bottom right photograph, Castelluccian ceramic fragments. Scale = 10 mm

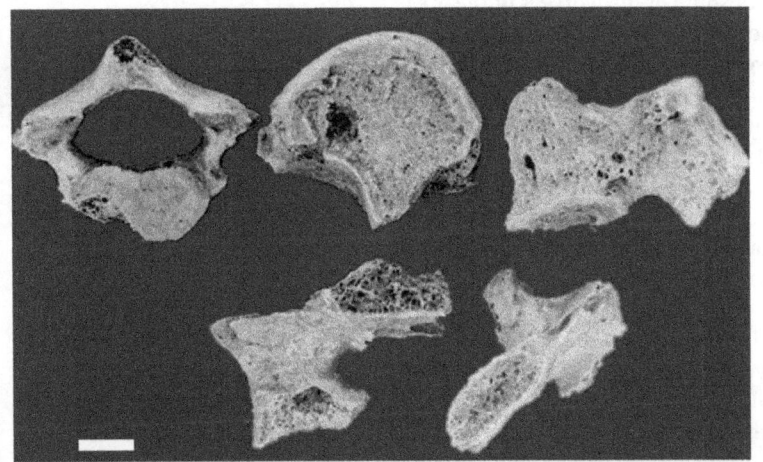

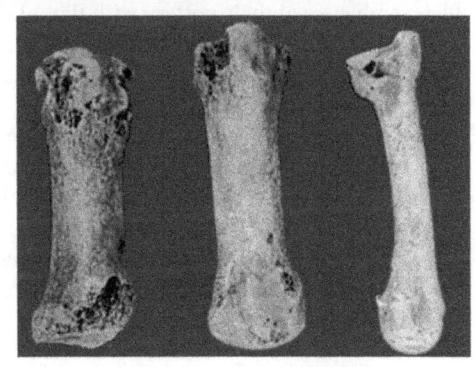
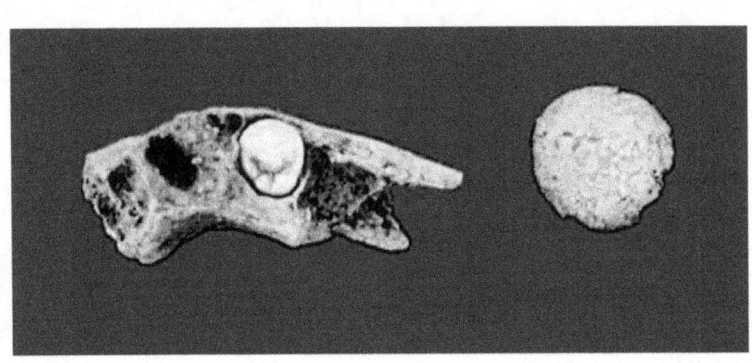

a farfetched hypothesis if you listen to the tales of some of the workers of the area: some years before my reconnaissance exploration, a large number of those tombs, complete with skeletons and funeral dowries, were wrecked and dispersed by the violent action of bulldozers employed for the construction of a road alongside the nature reserve. Irreparable damage was done. It will have deprived us of very much data together with making things difficult for us to compare specimens with some existing dolmens in the Iberian Peninsula, in Sardinia and in Apulia that had been built in the same way.

Structures that have been found in nearby Malta also lead us to suppose a common origin of the phenomenon. The mystery that hangs over the *Sicilian dolmen builders* could be revealed right here.

The advanced *Tarxien Civilisation*[16] of the little archipelago in the south of Sicily suddenly disappeared around four thousand five hundred years ago. Themistocles Zammit, a Maltese archaeologist of the early 1900s, hypothesizes the exceptional event was perhaps, indeed probably, due to a devastating plague that wiped out the inhabitants of the small islands: another ethnic group arrived there many centuries later. The traces of the *new population*, however, came to light immediately after the first. These traces were first encountered in the *Tarxien* "cremation cemetery", hence the name *Cemetery Culture of Tarxien*.

There must have been a good and proper invasion therefore, perpetrated by people who at first were thought to have come from the Aeolian Islands, due to the resemblance of their pottery with that of *Capo Graziano*[17]. However, we do not find the more elaborate vase shapes of the *Tarxien Cemetery* in Lipari and, moreover, the decorations are different[18]. This would exclude the invaders being from there.

The finding of some *Tarxien Cemetery* style pottery inside two Maltese dolmens (an architectural design foreign to the Aeolians), was part of putting an end to the doubt, once and for all, that the people came from the Aeolian Islands. Hence, the small megaliths of Malta and Gozo are attributed to the people of the *Tarxien Cemetery*[19]. The fact that these monuments were used as tombs though remains but a guess, perhaps becoming a certainty after the discoveries of the *Cava dei Servi* dolmen, the shape of which, moreover, brings to mind similar structures present in a vast area of the Mediterranean.

Technical data sheet of the monument

Height of lower slab	(1st on right)	0.89 metres
Width of lower slab	(1st on right)	0.89 metres
Thickness of lower slab	(1st on right)	0.22 metres
Height of lower slab	(2nd on right)	0.99 metres
Width of lower slab	(2nd on right)	0.61 metres
Thickness of lower slab	(2nd on right)	0.28 metres
Height of lower slab	(3rd on right)	0.88 metres
Width of lower slab	(3rd on right)	1.08 metres
Thickness of lower slab	(3rd on right)	0.20 metres
Height of lower slab	(4th on right)	0.93 metres
Width of lower slab	(4th on right)	0.88 metres

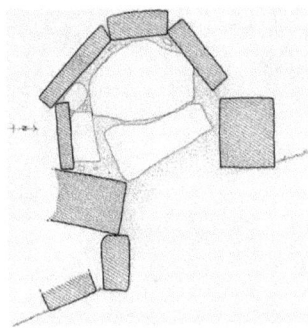

Cava dei Servi dolmen (ground plan)

Thickness of lower slab	(4th on right)	0.18 metres
Length of upper slab	(1st on right)	0.85 metres
Width of upper slab	(1st on right)	0.69 metres
Thickness of upper slab	(1st on right)	0.20 metres
Length of upper slab	(2nd on right)	0.46 metres
Width of upper slab	(2nd on right)	0.43 metres
Thickness of upper slab	(2nd on right)	0.19 metres
Length of upper slab	(3rd on right)	0.63 metres
Width of upper slab	(3rd on right)	1.15 metres
Thickness of upper slab	(3rd on right)	0.20 metres
Height of front right block		1.17 metres
Width of front right block		0.77 metres
Thickness of front right block		0.62 metres
Height of front left block		0.80 metres
Width of front left block		0.60 metres
Thickness of front left block		0.80 metres
Orientation (opening)		65° NE

Geographical map reference I.G.M. 1/25.000 – F° 276 I NE

Inventory of the human remains found underneath the large slab of the "Cava dei Servi" dolmen

4 incisors, 1 premolar & 3 molars; The eight teeth are perfectly preserved, with the protective enamel unaltered; the rounding of the molar bases and the wear on the walls of the incisors indicates they belonged to a rather mature individual;
1 right jaw fragment of an infant, with premolar not yet cut through the gum of the jaw border;
1 infant vertebral disk;
1 adult body vertebra;
1 almost complete adult cervical vertebra;
3 vertebra fragments in different places;
5 cranium fragments;
1 kneecap;
3 metapodials, of which 1 metatarsal and 2 metacarpals;
1 scapula fragment;
2 hip fragments;
1 ulna diaphisis fragment;
2 tibia fragments;
1 fibula diaphisis fragment;
1 hip fragment (iliac crest);
3 shapeless crude clay fragments, from a coarse wad and with traces of red ochre on the surfaces, relative to the Castelluccian Age.

Cava Lazzaro

The minor road from Pernicella to Marchesa, which is off from the right of the main Rosolini – Modica road after 8 km, leads to flatlands above a *Cava* (known as the Great Cava). The quarry cuts deeply and sinuously into part of the Rosolini territory. The first stretch, named *Cava Lazzaro*, is part of the southern Iblean highlands. Deep cracks have been worn into the rock by thousands of years of waterway incisions. Refuge and nutrition has always been found in such naturally forged places.

Going down the right slope of the Cava, via the short and steep natural terraces, the rocky walls seem to be pitted with *small artificial grotto* tombs, *oven* tombs, *vault* tombs with a hallway chamber, all of which dating back to the *Castelluccian facies*[20].

Ever since the second half of the 1800's, the area has revealed a considerable amount of prehistoric evidence. *Ferdinand von Andrian-Werburg*, the German anthropologist, is to be thanked for the explorations he led. In one of the many inside caverns, he found various artefacts in stone, some ceramic fragments dating back to the early Bronze Age and lots of bone remains, both human and those of different types of animal[21]. Great surprise arose from the finding of a human frontal, the curve of which was similar in form to the *Neanderthal* skull, along with an *axe* in lava material[22], similar to those come across in faraway Ireland[23].

The famous "Prince's Tomb" is on the same terrace, dug into the chalky rock. It has a monumental façade of eight false semi-columns with a double herringbone pattern, circular[24] and triangular embossment incisions[25]. It was from the *Grotta Lazzaro*[26], previously investigated by *von Andrian*, one of the enigmatic *globuled*

Prince's Tomb (Cava Lazzaro, Syracuse)

The Cava Lazzaro dolmen (Syracuse)

bones[27] came. *Tusa* suggests these could have been knife handles[28].

I went to this impressive place intrigued by the few lines recorded in the book of a scholar from Syracuse who alleged the presence of a "megalithic monument". Furthermore, the indications were illustrated with a poor photograph[29]. The presumed *dolmen*, rising just to the west of the *Prince's Tomb,* there and then leaves you somewhat perplexed, though showing glimpses of ruins of enormous stone buildings that had rolled along the slopes of the hill and massed together in the same point. In fact, pushing my way some few hundred metres west of the "pile-up", pointed out by *Belgiorno*, I localised two vertical columns that would have been the central part of a structure similar to the one of *Cava dei Servi*.

Here, instead of slabs, two large blocks of grey-white limestone from the area had been used and placed in such a way to sculpt a semi-circular form to the construction.

The surviving boulders, drafted using a club, rest on the chalky ground, typical of the area. The existence of hard sub-strata obliged the use of wide-based blocks, upheld by the different levels of the terrain. In fact, the back of both stones is only visible for a quarter of their height: a well-proven method, as we have already seen, which made it easier to cover the whole structure with earth and mud. The difference in thickness noted in one of the monoliths has been caused by atmospheric conditions which affect that side rather than the other.

The mastery of man is to be commended if you notice the conformation at the base of the left block. Our ancestors were able to solve the difference by inserting two wedge stones that were well-modelled to fit the purpose of keeping the defective element upright. An oblique groove runs along the surfaces of both boulders (you can only just see the aforementioned incision on the right block as it is less well-preserved than the other). This ridge, which was probably also on those stones that have been lost, makes us think that there were other slabs that had been systematically positioned obliquely to reduce the cap of the surface, in order to create a *false dome*.

The size of the cell is quite difficult to define though following a hypothetical curvature we could conclude an area of about 4 m².

Fragments of what may have been a *funereal construction* are still in a circle. A very large rounded stone on the left of the two vertical ones will have been part of the roof.

The ruins were discovered again some years after my investigative visit by the architect *Giuseppe Libra*[30], an archaeology enthusiast. He reached similar conclusions to those I had arrived at[31]. Doctor Libra did more though. He found a circular enclosure of stones around the two monoliths, which remind us of the characteristics of many Atlantic and Mediterranean dolmens (Holland, Spain, Corsica, Sardinia, Apulia and Malta).

This style of construction, already analysed more to the north in *Cava dei Servi*, repeats the work of one and the same population widespread throughout the Iblean highlands. These people lived alongside another *ethnic group*, the one that elaborated and used the tombs in the rock. Both peoples jealously held on to the products of their own traditions.

The absence of elements that help the dating of the monument does not allow us to understand the age of it. However, its correspondence to the one we analysed in the previous paragraph encourages us to believe it is an artefact that goes back to the third or the primordial years of the second millennium BC; a phase of the early *Bronze Age*.

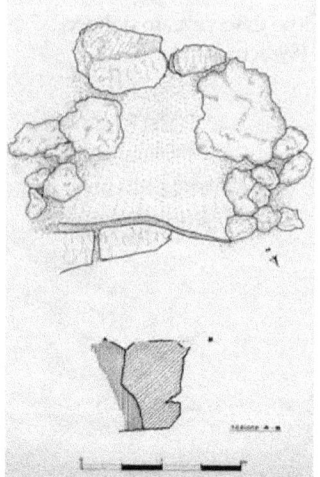

Cava Lazzaro dolmen (ground plan)

Technical data sheet of the monument

Height right monolith	1.06 metres
Width right monolith	0.84 metres
Thickness right monolith	0.75 metres
Height left monolith	1.06 metres
Width left monolith	0.76 metres
Thickness left monolith	0.37 metres

Geographical map reference I.G.M. 1/25.000 – F° 276 I SE

The pseudo dolmen of Avola

Avola is a big coastal city which lies between the River *Assinaro* and River *Cassibile*, some twenty kilometres south of Syracuse on the eastern coast of the island.

No literary source mentions what might have been one of the most ancient cities of Sicily, where, in and around the immediate territory, archaeological evidence of quite remote times can be found. Traces that back up the theory are present on the mountain above[32], where the mediaeval city stood before an earthquake destroyed it in 1693, so being abandoned for the present site. Greco-Roman

The Avola "dolmen" (Syracuse)

statuettes[33], ruins of a first century BC villa[34] and numerous *Christian Hypogeum*[35] have come to light.

Along the main road that goes to Syracuse, to the right of the Avola City Hospital a somewhat narrow track opens up and runs along a bed of a torrent. The slow process of waterway erosion has outlined a valley there, called *Cava L'Unica*. It is here on the right under a low rock face the presumable megalithic monument is situated. This area which is outside of the city centre is indicated with the name *Contrada Borgellusa*.

The dolmen, discovered by a teacher from Avola, *Salvatore Ciancio* in 1961, was covered with earth in such a way to seem part of the rock. The semblance of an entrance had always given the idea of a cave.

Professor Ciancio ended up convinced he had come across an ancient artefact, after he had carefully examined the ravine, and that it risked remaining hidden away from study. The credibility and seriousness of the researcher convinced the administrators of the local authorities of the time to clear the area near the structure, so freeing a literally unique *architectural structure* from under the heap that had built up over the centuries. Strong discussion arose between Salvatore Ciancio, who was certain it was a *megalith*, and the official science of the time.

The civic Assembly of Avola, confiding in the documentation of their illustrious citizen, thought well to fence off and prohibit access to the area to avoid any unlawful building speculation, or intrusion, damaging the find. Unfortunately, at that time much uncontrollable and illegal construction was being carried out

The Avola "dolmen". Detail of the left pillar

even in places that were known to be rich in archaeological sites. The press gave a lot of coverage and importance to the discovery, reporting the visits of important archaeologists to the so-called dolmen in great detail.

Visits followed from *Luigi Bernabò Brea*, the then Superintendent of Monuments and Fine Arts, Syracuse, and *Giorgio Vinicio Gentili* an inspector of the same organisation. They were inclined to have many doubts, as picked up from press reports. The same doubts were held by *Giuseppe* and *Santi Luigi Agnello*[36], and *Paolo Griffo*, the Superintendent of Agrigento.

Giuseppe Laghi, a Dominican monk and lecturer in the History of Art at Florence University, was among others who visited too. He showed great interest in the "monument" promising to go into the studies. *Daniel F. McCall,* Rector of the Faculty of Ethnology, Boston University, who visited in 1964, came to the conclusion that the characteristic *construction* could have been rightly listed as a *Megalithic work*[37].

The building which today is surrounded by thick and wild vegetation seems, at first sight, to be made of one enormous "chalk slab" of varying thickness, essentially placed on two "pillars". Fracturing of the stone necessitated the erection of three brick supports. The work was carried out by the local authorities. The stone is really huge with a corrugated surface. It is almost eight metres in length and five and a half metres in width.

The north-facing part of the platform, which seems to be resting on one isolated and irregular-shaped pillar stone, is more compact. It thins down to approximately half a metre in thickness at the eastern part which, in turn, rests on what could be called a very wide earthen base.

The rock wall behind, from which the enormous slab has objectively broken off because of a fracture line, blocks, in a south-westerly direction, the back part in a semi-circle. The left "pillar" is connected to this wall.

On the surface of the slab, which is broken in two places, ten small rectangular hollows are to be seen. They were worked into the thicker part of the flattish stone, in different directions so that they would not weaken it. The niches are of different lengths, ranging between sixty centimetres and one metre twenty of the last hollow, which is interrupted by the fracture of the southern extremity. The depth does not exceed forty centimetres.

We are perhaps in front of a tomb for children, used in *Greek* or *Paleochristian* times. At the time of his discovery, *Ciancio* found no element to date the construction. But, considering the aversion of early Christians towards burying their dead in places that were easy to find, due to the fact that they were more exposed to plunder, he deduced it was used in the Greek period.

Two grooves run along the outmost eastern side of the slab and they meet at a right-angle. Certain fantastic "literature" of the period came to the conclusion that these two incisions could be defined as draining lines for the blood of sacrifice victims to run along. Instead, they are notches resulting from the extraction of a block of limestone, of about one cubic metre, drawn from the point where the thickness was fitting.

A cavern of 30 m² opens up underneath the platform. It is open on two sides (north-west and north-east) and a little more than a metre and a half in height.

The error of speaking too soon might have been the result of just a superficial look at the structure. However, this was avoided with the help of the geologist Doctor *Giuseppe Ansaldi* whose technical judgement brings us to the prologue and, at the same time, the wish to investigate at 360°:

> "We are looking at a small grotto that was cut out of Pleistocene chalk by marine abrasion. The site comprises alternating strata of a more substantial competence, between 0.50 and 1.20 metres in thickness, with layers of gritty sand, some centimetres thick.
>
> The wall follows a discontinuous line facing NW-SE, along which, at this point, there is river erosion.
>
> There are also minor faults and veins that derive from a sub-perpendicular system to the one described; N 30°- 35° E direction.
>
> The intersection of the two discontinuous lines, easy to see on the front face , has dismembered the rock in contiguous blocks of differing volume. Influenced by these geomorphic elements, both fluvial and marine abrasive erosion has taken place.
>
> The formation of the cavity is the result of selective erosive action of the rock, with a more rapid and intense cutting away of the softer basal part (decimetre strata of gritty sand), up to contact with the bank above it which is more compact and resistant, so acting as the roof of the cavity.
>
> The continuing action of erosive processes, rifts, seismic events and Bradisism, involving the area in question, have brought to light submerged settlements and handicrafts of historic and prehistoric eras. Moreover, they caused the detachment of the cavity from the rock wall. It underwent roto-translation downhill with a large breach opening upstream and a tilting of the vault support to the right, as can be seen by the accentuated anomalous

dipping of the gritty sand strata it comprises.

The breaking away of the cavity from the wall is chronologically later than the pre-existing tombs made on the surface of the bank overlapping it. This is clearly shown by the fact that the breach produced on the wall snapped some of the existing sepulchral cells on the upper surface of the overhead bank.

With the back-up of observations carried out, there is no doubt this is a natural form of erosion, which is quite frequent along coastal cliffs and river valley banks.

It is equally evident that in prehistoric times the original natural form was reshaped by the hand of man following the natural lines of the boulder, intending to amplify and geometrically refine the cavity to its present appearance. Traces of such intervention are visible both around the pillars taken from the side walls of the grotto, giving them a pseudo-parallelepiped form, and in the flat surface of the calcarenite vault. The base of the vault has been cleared of underlying sandy-arenite materials, following the surface of lower stratification."

The geologist's analysis, therefore, does not preclude the intervention of man on a natural fixture that might have been adapted to *experimental architectural elaboration.* Perhaps the intervention was for dwelling purposes, though impeded somewhat by its structural appearance: the side openings are incompatible to the logic of a domestic refuge. If an occasional refuge was to be contemplated, the work performed by humans has made it so vulnerable that this possibility of "shelter" is just not logical.

The expedient, instead, seems to be an effort to "monumentalise" a structure provided by Nature, saving man from the bulk of the work. It can be compared to any well-thought out Megalithic construction in Atlantic Europe.

The Solarino dolmen, lost now (Syracuse)

Pseudo dolmen of Avola (plan)

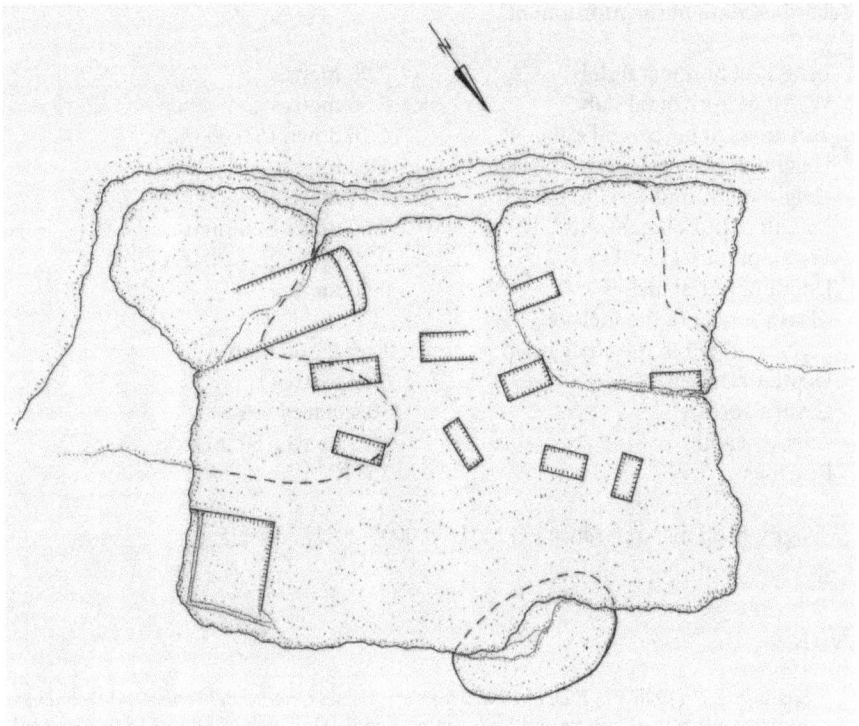

South-eastern Sicily has been witness to the dolmen phenomena, as attested by the numerous reports between 1960-1980, indicating *Giarratana*, *Marina di Modica* and *Noto*. An exceptionally large trilithic (three-stone) construction was found in Belvedere, a panoramic area above Syracuse.

Other traces came to light in Solarino, near the *Corruggi* manor farm: four vertical stones in a circle, little more than one metre high, bore a boulder which served as a cover. The shape of the building, according to Professor Rodolfo Striccoli, lecturer of Prehistory and Protohistory at Bari University, was reminiscent of a well-known dolmen typology present in Apulia[38]. There is nothing remaining of the ruin as it was covered by tons of earth during work on an enormous dam for hydro-electric power in that very place. Similar constructions are claimed to have been on that site too. A megalithic work also existed near the River Mulinello, in *Villasmundo* (Melilli), in the *Petraro* district.

Just a few faded photographs remain as witness to its presence. They show an enormous block which had once been fitted onto two vertical stones, remaining so fixed only on one column as the other must have accidentally slid on land that had been beaten by centuries of weathering.

Returning to the "pseudo" dolmen of Avola, it is opportune to clarify that there is no intention to justify its *status* through simple analyses of the exterior, nor though, is it wise to consider the archaeological investigations superfluous. On the contrary, we must be convinced of the opportune incontrovertible action of the pickaxe, in order to solve a doubt that has been there for more than forty years.

Technical data of the monument

Length of horizontal slab	7.90 metres
Width of horizontal slab	5.50 metres
Thickness of horizontal slab	1.70 down to 0.60 metres
Height of ground-level to the right	1.12 metres
Height of ground-level to the left	1.47 metres
Length of burial niches (N°. 10)	0.60 up to 1.20 metres
Width of burial niches	0.26 up to 0.54 metres
Depth of burial niches	0.40 metres
Measurement of the incision carried out in the chalky slab	1.00 x 1.00 metres
Depth of the cut	0.60 metres
Cavern surface	30 square metres
Cavity height	1.45 up to 1.50 metres
Bearings	35° NE

Geographical map reference I.G.M. 1/25.000 – F° 277 IV NE

Notes

[1] Spadafora, S. (1996-97) *Il Dolmen di Mura Pregne nel Quadro del Fenomeno Dolmenico Europeo,* Faculty of Letters and Philosophy, Scuola Universitaria diretta a fini Speciali per Operatori Tecnico-scientifici per i beni Culturali ed Ambientali, settore Archeologico, 48-65, Thesis, Palermo University.

[2] Orsi, P. (Pancucci, D. Ed.) (1972-73) *Esplorazioni a Monte Bubbonia dal 1904 al 1906,* Archivio Storico Siracusano, n.s. **II**, Siracusa.

[3] Herodotus, **VII**, 153, 2; cf. Orlandini, P. (1961) *Omphake and Maktorion,* Kokalos **VII**, page 165 onwards.

[4] Orsi, P. (Pancucci, D. Ed.) (1972-73) *Esplorazioni a Monte Bubbonia dal 1904 al 1906,* Archivio Storico Siracusano, n.s. **II**, 46, Siracusa.

[5] *Sicilia Archeologica* (1983) 52-53, **XVI**, 71.

[6] Pancucci, D. & Naro, M.C. (1992) *Monte Bubbonia, compagne di scavo, 1905, 1906, 1955,* in: Collana di monografie pubblicate dal Centro di studi storico-archeologici "Biagio Pace", p. 151.

[7] Pancucci, D. (1973) *Monte Bubbonia,* Sicilia Archeologica, **23**, 55 [Pantalica, clinging to the inland highlands of the Province of Syracuse, dominating the valley of the River Anapo, between the cities of Sortino and Ferla, gives its name to the final phase of the Sicilian Bronze Age. This era is subdivided into four periods between *circa* 1270 BC and 650 BC].

[8] Orsi, P. & D. Pancucci (1972-73) *Esplorazioni a Monte Bubbonia dal 1904 al 1906,* Archivio Storico Siracusano, n.s. **II**, Siracusa.

[9] Del Campo, M. & Scrofani, G. (1971) *Insediamenti preistorici nella Cava dei Servi,* in: Un quinquennio di attività archeologica nella provincia di Siracusa, pp. 20-21.

[10] Di Stefano, G. (1984) *Piccola guida delle stazioni preistoriche degli Iblei,* Distretto scolastico 52, pp. 85 onwards, Ragusa.

[11] Di Stefano, G. *Cava dei Servi,* Studi Etruschi, vol. **XLVI** (III series), 577.

[12] Guzzardi, L. (1996) *L'area degli Iblei fra l'età del bronzo e la prima età del ferro,* in: Civiltà indigene e città Greche nella regione iblea; Guzzardi, L. Ed. *Assessorato*

[13] *BB.CC.AA. della Regione Siciliana e Distretto scolastico* 52, p. 17.
The skeletal remains belonged to two individuals, one adult and the other still a youngster. Owing to the unusual thickness, the cranial fragments have diagnostically resulted in showing the adult suffered a clinical pathology that was fairly common in the mediterranean area - thalassaemia (Mediterranean anaemia).

[14] *The Culture of Castelluccio* (from the name of the site situated some twenty kilometres from Noto), goes back to the first phase of the Bronze Age (*Early Bronze Age*). It would seem the population of *Castelluccio* came from central Anatolia, because of the evident similarities between Sicilian pottery of this Sicilian cultural facies and its contemporary in the Middle-East, called "Cappadocia"; cf. Bernabò Brea, L. (1958) *La Sicilia prima dei Greci*, pp.109-110, Milan.

[15] Di Stefano, G. (1979) *La collezione preistorica della "Grotta Lazzaro" nel museo civico di Modica*, Sicilia Archeologica, 41, 108; cf. also Orsi, P. (1898) *Miniere di selce e sepolcri eneolitici a Monte Tabuto e Monte Racello presso Comiso (Siracusa)*, Bullettino di Paletnologia Italiana, **XXIV**, 203.

[16] Locality in the east of Malta, dug out from the Zammit between 1915 and 1917. We are dealing with a complex of four temples that cover an area of 5,300 sq. ms., inside of which the lower half of a gigantic statue representing the local divinity was found. The Bronze Age invaders used the ruins of the previous temples as a cremation necropolis. Other minor temple complexes are to be found in *Hagiar Kim, Mnaidra, Mgiarr, Sorba* on the main island, and *Gigantija* in Gozo.

[17] A village situated on the headland of the same name on Filicudi, an Aeolian island, from which a *Culture* of the Early Bronze Age takes its name. A rather coarse type of pottery characterises it. The ceramics are decorated with interspersed linear incisions, sometimes from patterns, either geometrical or floral, which are got from pressing the artefact while still humid.

[18] Evans, J. D. (1961) *Segreti dell'Antica Malta*, pages 177 onwards, Milan.

[19] Cf. Evans, J. D. (1961) *Segreti dell'Antica Malta*, p. 176, Milan.

[20] Di Stefano, G. (1976) *Nuovissimi documenti tombali della prima età del bronzo a "Cava Lazzaro"*, Tabellarius, n.s., 12 on; cf. also Picone, E.G. (2006) *Stanziamenti preistorici nel territorio dell'alta Cava d'Ispica*, pp. 40-45, Siracusa.

[21] Andrian [von], F. (1878) *Präistoriche studien aus Sicilien*, Zeitschrift für Ethnologie, **X**, 79-82, Berlin.

[22] Pigorini, L. (1882) Scoperte paletnologiche nel territorio di Modica. *Bullettino Di Paletnologia Italiana*, **8**, 21-25.

[23] Axes with the edge facing upwards were found in *Carnac*, Brittany, in one of the many dolmen of that place. Under the so-called *Merchants' Table* in Locmariaquer, very near Carnac, a sculpted axe-plough figure can be seen, and in Manéer Hroec, Brittany, a perforated disklike jadeite axe was brought to light inside a Megalithic cell, as well as about a hundred axes tied up in bundles placed one above the other (cf. Galles, R. [1863] *Bull. Soc. Polym. Morbihan*, **VIII**, 2). Axes are also sculpted in the Megalithic complex of *Stonehenge*.

[24] Orsi, P. (1906) *Nuovi documenti della civiltà premicenea e micenea in Italia*, Ausonia, Year **1**, 7 on.

[25] For this last decorative motif, cf. Libra, G. (2006) *Quei sei triangoli equilateri*, in: Le Timpe, Libro Antologico, pp. 69-71, Rosolini.

[26] Grotta Lazzaro, which takes its name from the quarry where it is to be found, is a cavern of Carsic (an arid stone, though not sterile) nature used as a refuge since the upper Paleolithic period (circ. 35,000 years ago).

[27] Maugini, F. (1879) *Scoperte preistoriche in Sicilia*, Rivista scientifica industriale; cf. also Orsi, P. (1906) *Nuovi documenti della civiltà premicenea e micenea in Italia*, Ausonia, Year **1**, 5-6. ["Globuled bones" are small plates of bovine bone, finely decorated with embossed motifs that reproduce "oval globules" placed in a row. The Sicilian examples were found in the necropolises of *Castelluccio*, in *Cava Lazzaro*, in *Sante Croci*, in

Monte Casale and in the Masella grotto, Buscemi. Others cropped up in the II and III levels (2700-2300 B.C.) of *Troy*, in *Malta*, in *Lerna* and in the *Peloponnese* in the strata that refers to the Middle Helladic period (2000-1580 BC)].

[28] Tusa, S. (1983) *La Sicilia nella preistoria*, p. 320, Palermo.

[29] Belgiorno, F. L. (1965) *I Siciliani di 15,000 anni fa*, p. 120, Catania.

[30] Libra, G. *Identificato un dolmen a Cava Lazzaro*, in: Le Timpe, Libro Antologico, pp. 73-75, Rosolini.

[31] Piccolo, S. (1995) *I dolmen nella Sicilia sud-orientale*, Faculty of Letters and Philosophy, Scuola Universitaria diretta a fini speciali per Operatori Tecnico-Scientifici per i beni Culturali ed Ambientali, settore Archeologico, 61-67, Thesis, Palermo University.

[32] Orsi, P. (1899) *Avola. Sepolcri siculi e catacombe cristiane*, Notizie Scavi di antichità, 69-70.

[33] Gentili, G.V. (1954 [1956]), *Fasti archeologici* **IX**, n.r. 2792.

[34] Currò, M. T. (1966) *Avola. Casa romana in contrada Borgellusa*, Bollettino D'Arte, **LI**, 94; cf. also Bacci, G.M. (1984/1985) *Avola (1980-1983). Villa ellenistico-romana in contrada Borgellusa*, Kokalos, **II**, pages 711 onwards.

[35] Albanese, R. M. (1978) *Notiziario, Avola*, Studi Etruschi, **XLVI**, 569-571.

[36] Father and son, both renowned lecturers of Christian Archaeology at Catania University.

[37] Piccolo, S. (1995) *I dolmen nella Sicilia sud-orientale*, Faculty of Letters and Philosophy, Scuola Universitaria diretta a fini speciali per Operatori Tecnico-Scientifici per i beni Culturali ed Ambientali, settore Archeologico, plate XVIII, Thesis, Palermo University.

[38] *Le ruspe travolgono un prezioso dolmen*, La Domenica, a Syracuse weekly (25th September 1983).

3 Umbilicus Mundi

Epilogue

The interpretation of those artefacts that have just been discussed seems to open up new horizons on the composite cultural panorama of primitive Sicily. It is a well-known fact that this region went through a quite intricate prehistory, so much so it is difficult to move about in the muddle of peoples that have followed each other. The impact of two influences, however, remains clear: the European one coming from the North-West, and the other, the Mediterranean influence, of a clear oriental matrix.

When in the VIII century BC the first Aegean colonies reached in this country, the island was inhabited by three indigenous progenies: the Sicanians, the Siculo people and the Elimi[1]. Written witness to their origins is extremely confused, and a peremptory ethnic identification with the Greeks would tend to limit, if not conclude, the framework of the investigation.

The "Billella" dolmen in Lùras (Sassari)

The "Alzoleddha" dolmen in Lùras, Sassari

Once ascertained the non-involvement of dolmen architecture and those would-be last *cultures* of prehistoric Sicily, we are left with turning our attention to a further experience which evolved here during the *Metal age*.

Megalithism, as we have mentioned more than once, is mainly concentrated in the European Atlantic area, following a course that seems to go back down the continent from North (England, Brittany) towards south (Portugal, Spain).

Around the end of the III millennium BC, the west coast of Sicily was caught up in a cultural wave (bringing the bell-shaped goblet[2]) coming from the Sardinian coast. The effects of this determined the creation of a mercantile coupling, even in the south-west of the island[3], with the purpose of regulating traffic between central-south Sicily, Sardinia and the Iberian Peninsula on one side and the east Mediterranean on the other[4]. This would thus explain the passage of typical cultural aspects of Western Europe through the Sicily of the time that, apart from creating local imitation phenomena[5], testified the strategic/commercial centrality of this land. Sardinia, due to its geographic position, had to act as the last "service station" of that long virtual bridge that connected the opposite shores of the Mediterranean.

There is a high Megalithic concentration in the small community of Lùras, near Sassari. It is possible to view two rectangular-shaped dolmens with their entrances facing north-east. They are named Billella and Alzoleddha[6]. The former, 2.00 x 1.70 x 1.70 m, has a cover slab measuring 2.2 x 2.3 m; the latter, no higher than one metre, is made up of three big granite slabs. They are fixed in the ground and capped by a slab of 2.65 x 2.20 m. Both of them are to be dated back to the Bronze Age.

Similar structures are to be found in Spongano, in the Province of Lecce. Not more than a few years ago was the umpteenth dolmen found and named *Piedi grandi* (*Big Feet*) after the base on which it was built. Dating back to the first half of the second millennium BC it consists of two stones that were stuck into the ground and topped with a quadrangular slab, with rounded corners, 1.10 m in width.

The monument is about ninety centimetres high, of the same width and only one metre deep. The afore-mentioned artefacts are similar to our Monte Bubbonia example in a decisive manner; in form, dimension and orientation.

The "pseudo dolmen" of Avola remains isolated in this panorama, as, having ascertained its natural conformation, its construction style distances it from the before described examples.

When, in 1955, J.D. Evans, in the mentioned work, attributed the construction of the small megaliths from Malta to a people from Apulia he did not yet know of the Sicilian dolmen scenario. It would seem reductive to reiterate the hypothesis of the English academic referring only to the formal aspect of the monuments of the two regions, especially if, in the meantime, a third one is interposed and claims similar experiences. Above all, the dating of the artefacts from Apulia (not validated by any chronological element, either absolute or relative) is later than that indicated for those verified in Malta.

Sicily, because of her geographic impressiveness right in the middle of the Mediterranean, attracted every type of cultural experience, passing on the effects to those areas that were influence, both to the north and the south.

The age-old connections with the island of Malta are pictured in this framework, thus asserting a privileged partnership with the big sister yet always on the alert of a proximity that could prove dangerous.

The making of progress of metallurgy did not in any way undermine the role

The "Piedi Grandi" dolmen at Spongano (Lecce)

of Sicily, on the contrary it opened the doors to the West and took so-far unseen models and raw materials. Arsenic[7] came from Sardinia and, via the same route, tin arrived from Spain and Cornwall.

The "dolmen people" will have taken part in that coming and going. Landing in the east of this region, they had to expand little by little towards the Ionian coast, ending up taking advantage of the virtuous circuit that this part of the island had triggered off some time before with the Maltese archipelago. Maybe it was here the Tarxien civilisation met its sad end.

Notes

[1] Thucydides **VI**, 2.
[2] *The bell-shaped mug* appeared in Sicily back in the Copper Age, being fully asserted in the period at the turn with the Bronze Age (around 2200 BC). The importance of the drinking vessel is in the frequency it has been found in a very vast area of the European continent, from Portugal to Scotland, from Spain to Alsace, to Bohemia.
[3] The other Sicilian commercial port of call, very much older, is in the north-east, in the Aeolian islands.
[4] Tusa, S. (1994) *Sicilia Preistorica*, pp. 121 onwards, Palermo.
[5] For example, pottery in the Castelluccian style of Manicalunga (near Trapani) is affected by the decorative influence of the bell-shaped mug; the *polypode* vases (from Gk polypodes, "with more feet") found in this part of Sicily, show evident affinity to those come across in many areas of central Europe; the small grotto tomb found on Sicilian territory, acquires an element of distinction due to the addition of a "dolmen corridor"; cf. Tusa, S. (1994) *Sicilia preistorica*, p. 119, Palermo; Castellana, G. (2002) *La Sicilia nel II millennio*, pp. 105 on, Caltanissetta.
[6] The names of two districts in Lùras: *Billella*, in the adjoining countryside; *Alzoleddha*, instead, within the urban area.
[7] Arsenic, a semi-metal used as an antifriction alloy component which improved the sturdiness of works in copper. It was progressively abandoned as bronze fusion procedures were perfected (a phase of the *Mid-Bronze Age*, around 1500 BC).

Chronology of Sicilian Prehistory

Neolithic (6000–3000 BC)

4800–3700 BC Stentinello Culture
Pottery decorated with impressions or incisions made in the clay prior to firing. The decorations, very rough, were often made with fingernails or a range of punches and occasionally with the edges of shells (Cardium or Pectunculus). Other examples consist of incised lines, forming shaded triangles. Ceramics include bowls, cups and fruit bowls with high feet, sometimes perforated.

3700–3000 BC Bichromic (Grotta delle Felci) and trichrome ceramics (Matrensa style)
Serra d'Alto style (spiral/meander decorations). Diana style (red or brown pottery decorated with wide furrows. Cylindrical handles).

Copper Age (3000–2169 BC)

3000–2600 BC San Cono/Piano Notaro Culture
Place of origin - Aegean Islands (Chios, Samos and Lesbos). Shepherd communities, nomads, hunters (underground tombs). Ceramics exhibiting a yellow background, small decorative embossed buttons, red stripes and black lines.

2600–2350 BC Serraferlicchio Culture
Ceramics with red background and black graphics. Geometric decorative syntax disordered.

2350–2150 BC Malpasso-Sant'Ippolito Culture
Early Aegean-Anatolians, monochrome ceramic red/glossy, dark background and pale designs.

Early Bronze Age (2169–1400 BC)

2169–1400 BC Castelluccio Culture
Red pottery, hand thrown and not turned, with black designs. Ordered decorative syntax (globular bones). Contact with the Aegean world (Greece and Turkey), matt painted ware. Contact with Malta. Presence of dolmens.

Middle Bronze Age (1400–1270 BC)

1400–1270 BC Thapsos Culture
Importation of bronze from Aegean area and from Cyprus. Unique fortified villages in Sicily: Thapsos, Villasmundo, Branco Grande (Vittoria/Comiso). In Thapsos the presence of tombs with Mycenaean pottery. Towns contain a range of dwellings from huts to brick houses aligned to arteries; the forerunner to centres of urban development.

Final Bronze Age (1270–1000 BC)

1270–650 BC Pantalica Culture
The withdrawal of the Sicanians, for defensive reasons, from the coastal towns to the interior of the island. Arrival of Sicels around 1270 BC. The final Bronze Age is divided by scholars into:

- Pantalica I (North) 1270–1000 BC;
- Pantalica II (Cassibile) 1000–850 BC, elbow fibula, feathered ceramics, geometric motifs replaced by floral;
- Pantalica III (South) 850–730 BC. Arrival of the first Greek colonies on the eastern shores of the island;
- Pantalica IV (Finocchito) 730–650 BC.

Bibliography

Anati, E. "Considerazioni sulla preistoria di Malta (nota preliminare)". In Anati, A.F. & Anati, E. (eds.), *Missione a Malta: Ricerche e Studi sulla Preistoria dell'arcipelago Maltese nel contesto Mediterraneo* 11–49. Milano: Jaca Book, 1988.
Arribas, A. *The Iberians*. London: Thames and Hudson, 1960.
Atkinsons, R.J.C. "Neolithic engineering". York: *Antiquity* **35** 292–299, 1961.
Bacchiega, M. *Validità ed Attualità del Mito Solare*. Lendinara (Rovigo): Vanzan, 1964.
Bandi, H.G. "La répartition des tombes mégalithiques". Genève: *Archives Suisse d'Anthropologie Générale* **12** 39–51, 1946.
Belgiorno, F.L. *I Siciliani di 15 Mila Anni Fa*. Catania: E.I.A, 1965.
Beltrán, A., Facchini, F., Kozlowski, J.K., Thomas, H. & Tobias, P.V. *Paleoantropologia e Preistoria (Origini, Paleolitico, Mesolitico)*. Milano: Jaca Book, 1993.
Bernabò Brea, L. *Sicily Before the Greeks*. New York: Frederick A. Preaeger, 1957.
Bernabò Brea, L, "Eolie, Sicilia e Malta nell'età del bronzo". *Kokalos* **22/23** 33–108, 1976/77.
Bernardini, E. "Europa megalitica". *Mondo Archeologico* 51–61. Firenze: Corrado Tedeschi Editore, 1977.
Bonanno, A. *Malta: an Archaeological Paradise*. Valletta: *MJ* Publications, 2000.
Bovio Marconi, J. "Termini Imerese (Monte Castellaccio). Relazione Preliminare". *Notizie degli Scavi di Antichità* 462–473, 1936.
Bradley, R. & Gardiner, J. (eds.) *Neolithic Studies: a Review of some Current Research*. Oxford: British Archaeological Reports, 1984.
Cantone, S. "Il dolmen di Sciacca". *Sicilia* **82** 19, 1977.
Castellana, G. *La Sicilia nel II Millennio a. C.* Caltanissetta: S. Sciascia, 2002.
Chapman, R. "The emergence of formal disposal areas and the "problem" of megalithic areas in prehistoric Europe". In Chapman, R., Kinnes, I. & Randsborg, K. (eds), *The Archaeology of Death*. Cambridge: Cambridge University Press, 1981.
Childe, V.G. *The Prehistory of European Society*. London: Cassell, 1962.
Cipolloni Sampò, M. *Dolmen. Architetture Preistoriche in Europa*. Roma: De Luca

Edizioni d'Arte, 1990.

Daniel, G.E. *The Megalith Builders of Western Europe*. London: Hutchinson & Co Ltd, 1958.

Daniel, G.E. & Kjaerum P. (eds.) *Megalithic Graves and Ritual: Papers Presented at the III Atlantic Colloqium, Moesgård 1969*. København: Jutland Archaeological Society Publication 11, Gyldendal, 1973.

Darvill, T. & Malone, C. (eds.) *Megaliths from Antiquity (Antiquity Papers, 3)*. Cambridge: Antiquity Publications, 2003.

Di Stefano, C.A. "L'ignoto centro archeologico di Mura Pregne presso Termini Imerese". *Kokalos* **XVI** 188–198, 1970.

Di Stefano, G. "Nuovissimi documenti tombali della prima età del bronzo a Cava Lazzaro". Ragusa: *Tabellarius, n.s.* 12–21, 1976.

Di Stefano, G. "La collezione preistorica della "Grotta Lazzaro" nel Museo civico di Modica". Roma: *Sicilia Archeologica* **41** 91–110, 1979.

Di Stefano, G. *Piccola Guida delle Stazioni Preistoriche degli Iblei*. Ragusa: Distretto scolastico 52, 1984.

Erasmus, C.J. "Monument building: some field experiments". Albuquerque: *Southwestern Journal of Anthropology* **21** 277–301, 1965.

Evans, J.D. "The "Dolmens" of Malta and the origins of the Tarxien cemetery culture". In *Proceedings of the Prehistoric Society* **22** 85–102, 1956.

Evans, J.D. *Malta*. London: Thames and Hudson, 1959.

Fleming, A. "The Myth of the Mother-goddess". London: *World Archaeology* **1** 247–261, 1969.

Fleming, A. "Tombs for the living". London: *Man* **8** 177–193, 1973.

Furon, R. *Manuel de Préhistoire Générale: Géologie et Biogéographie, Évolution de L'humanité, Archéologie Préhistorique, les Métaux et la Protohistoire*. Paris: Payot, 1958.

Gatti, E. *La misteriosa Civiltà dei Reti*. Roma: Cardini, 1972.

Gervasio, M. *I dolmen e la Civiltà del Bronzo nelle Puglie*. Trani: Ditta tipografica editrice Vecchi, 1913.

Guzzardi, L. "Architettura funeraria pluricellulare della Sicilia sud-orientale tra la tarda età del Rame e la prima età del Bronzo". In *Preistoria d'Italia alla Luce delle Ultime Scoperte* **4** 315 onwards, 1984.

Guzzardi, L. "L'area degli Iblei fra l'età del Bronzo e la prima età del Ferro". In Guzzardi, L. (a cura di), *Civiltà indigene e città greche nella regione iblea* 9–42, 1996.

Guzzardi, L. "L'area del Siracusano e l'arcipelago maltese nella Preistoria". In Bonanno A. & Militello, P. (eds.), *Malta in the Hibleans, the Hibleans in Malta. Proc. Int. Conference Catania 30 September, Sliema 10 November 2006*, 40–49, 2008.

Guzzardi, L. "Arcipelago maltese e regione iblea: rapporti e divergenze fra III e II millennio a.C." In Bondin, R. & Gringeri Pantano F. (eds.), *Sicily and Malta: The Islands of the Grand Tour* 11–23, 2007.

Heine-Geldern (von), R. "Die megalithen Südostasiens und ihre Bedeutung für die Klärung der megalithenfrage in Europa und Polynesien". Fribourg: *Anthropos* **23** 276–315, 1928.

Heine-Geldern (von), R. "Das megalith problem". In *Beiträge Österreichs zur*

Erforschung der Vergangenheit und kulturgeschichte der Menschheit 162–182, 1959.

Heizer, R. F. "Ancient heavy transport, methods and achievements". *Science* **153** 821–830, 1966.

Holloway, R., Juokowsky, M.S. & Lukesh, S. *La Muculufa, the Early Bronze Age Sanctuary.* Providence: Centre for Old World Archaeology and Art, 1990.

Joussaume, R. *Des Dolmens Pour les Morts: les Mégalithismes à travers le Monde.* Paris: Hachette, 1985.

Lilliu, G. "Il dolmen di Motorra". *Studi Sardi* **XX** 3-57, 1966.

Lo Porto, F. G. "Il "dolmen a galleria" di Giovinazzo". Roma: *Bullettino di Paletnologia Italiana* **XVIII** 137–180, 1967.

Lynch, F. "The use of the passage in certain passage graves as a mean of communication rather than access". In Daniel, G.E. & Kiaerum, P. (eds), *Megalithic Graves and Ritual: Papers presented at the III Atlantic Colloquium, Moesgård 1969*, 147–161. København: Jutland Archaeological Society Publication 11, Gyldendal, 1973.

MacKie, E. *The Megalith Builders.* Oxford: Phaidon, 1977.

Maringer, J. *Vorgeschichtliche Religion: Religion im Steinzeitlichen Europa.* Zurich: Benziger, 1956.

Mauceri, L. *Sopra un'Acropoli Pelasgica esistente nei dintorni di Termini Imerese.* Palermo: Tipi del "Giornale di Sicilia", 1896.

Miller, D. & Tilley, C.Y. (eds) *Ideology, Power and Prehistory.* Cambridge: Cambridge University Press, 1984.

Mohen, J. P. "Aux prises avec des pièrres de plusieurs dizaines de tonnes la construction des dolmens et menhirs au Néolithique". Dijon: *Les Dossiers d'Archéologie* **46** 58–67, 1980.

Müller, S. *L'Europe Préhistorique: Principes d'Archéologie Préhistorique.* Paris: J. Lamarre, 1907.

Niel, F. *La Civilisation des Mégalithes.* Paris: Plon, 1970.

Orsi, P. "Miniere di selce e sepolcri eneolitici a Monte Tabuto e Monte Racello presso Comiso (Siracusa)". Roma: *Bullettino di Paletnologia Italiana* **XXIV** 165–206, 1898.

Orsi, P. "Villaggio, officina litica e necropoli sicula del 1º periodo a Monte Sallia presso Canicarao (Comiso, prov. di Siracusa)". Roma: *Bullettino di Paletnologia Italiana* **XLIII** 3–26, 1923.

Patiri, G. "Le mura e le costruzioni ciclopiche della contrada Cortevecchia, in Termini Imerese". Firenze: *Archivio per l'Antropologia e l'Etnologia* **XXXVIII** 17–22, 1908.

Peete, T.E. *Rough Stone Monuments and their Builders.* London & New York: Harper & Brothers, 1912.

Pellegrini, E. "Il mondo delle pietre giganti". *Archeo* **98** 54–103, 1993.

Peroni, R. *Archeologia della Puglia Preistorica.* Roma: De Luca, 1967.

Piccolo, S. "I dolmen nella Sicilia sud-orientale". In Scuderi, A., Tusa, S. & Vintaloro, A. (a cura di), *Atti del I Congresso Internazionale di Preistoria e Protostoria Siciliane vol. B* 305–315, 2006.

Piccolo, S. "La tavola e la pietra". *Archeo* **166** 42 onwards, 1998.

Picone, E.G. *Stanziamenti Preistorici nel Territorio dell'Alta Cava d'Ispica.* Siracusa:

Lombardi, 2006.

Pignatello, G. *Guida di Avola.* Ispica: Tipografia Martorina, 1980.

Pigorini, L. "Monumenti megalitici in terra d'Otranto". Roma: *Bullettino di Paletnologia Italiana* **XXV** 178, 1899.

Pigorini, L. *Cinquanta anni di storia italiana:[1860-1910]/ pubblicazione fatta sotto gli auspici del governo per cura della R. Accademia dei Lincei* **II**. Milano: U. Hoepli, 1911.

Policastro, S. *De Veteribus Recentioribusque Rebus Siculis.* Catania: Accademia Internazionale Siculo-Normanna, 1976.

Raclet, G. *Les Mégalithes Mystérieux.* Paris: R. Laffont, 1981.

Recami, E., Mignosa, C. & Baldini L.R. "Nuovo contributo sulla preistoria della Sicilia". Roma: *Sicilia Archeologica* **52/53** 45–82, 1983.

Reden (von), S. *Die Megalith-Kulturen: Zeugnisse Einer Verschollenen Urreligion.* Köln: DuMont, 1982.

Renfrew, C. "Colonialism and megalithismus". York: *Antiquity* **41** 276–288, 1967.

Renfrew, C. "New configurations in old world chronology". London: *World Archaeology* **2** 199–211, 1970.

Renfrew, C. "The megalithic monuments of western Europe". In Evans, J.D., Cunliffe, B. & Renfrew, C.(eds), *Antiquity and man: essays in honour of Glyn Daniel* **II**, 1981.

Renfrew, C. *Before Civilization, the Radiocarbon Revolution and Prehistoric Europe.* London: Jonathan Cape, 1973.

Röder, J. *Pfhal und Menhir, Eine Vergleichende Vorgeschichtliche, Volks und Völkerkundliche Studie.* Neuwied: Jost, 1949.

Spadafora, S. *Il Dolmen di Mura Pregne nel Quadro del Fenomeno Dolmenico Europeo.* Thesis, University of Palermo: Faculty of Letters and Philosophy, Scuola Universitaria diretta a fini Speciali per Operatori Tecnico-scientifici per i beni Culturali ed Ambientali, settore Archeologico, A.Y. 1996–1997.

Thom, A. & Thom, A.S. *Megalithic Remains in Britain and Brittany.* Oxford: Clarendon Press, 1978.

Troia, S. *Avola alla Luce delle Scoperte Archeologiche: Testimonianze di Antiche Vestigia.* Moschiano (Avellino): M. Cozzo, 1963.

Troia, S. *Avola alla Luce della Storia e dell'Archeologia.* Noto: Ionica, 1963.

Trump, D.H. *Central and Southern Italy before Rome.* London: Thames and Hudson, 1966.

Trump, D.H. "Megalithic architecture in Malta". In Renfrew, C. (ed.), *The Megalithic Monuments of Western Europe* 64–77. London: Thames and Hudson, 1983.

Tusa, S. "The megalith builders and Sicily". Valletta: *Journal of Mediterranean Studies* **1/2** 267–285, 1991.

Tusa, S. *Sicilia Preistorica.* Palermo: D. Flaccovio, 1994.

Tusa, S. "Il megalitismo e la Sicilia". In S. Tusa (a cura di), *Prima Sicilia: Alle Origini della Società Siciliana* 333–341. Palermo: Ediprint, 1997.

Twohig, E.S. *The Megalithic Art of Western Europe.* Oxford: Clarendon Press, 1981.

Voza, G. "Villaggio fortificato dell'età del bronzo in Contrada Petraro di Melilli (Siracusa)". In *Atti della XII riunione scientifica, Palermo-Lipari, 22-26 Ottobre*

1967, 173–187, 1968.

Wernick, R. *The Monument Builders.* New York: Time-Life Books, 1973.

Whitehouse, R. "Megaliths of the central Mediterranean". In Renfrew, C. (ed.), *The Megalithic Monuments of Western Europe* 42–63. London: Thames and Hudson, 1983.

Whittle, A. *Problems in Neolithic Archaeology.* Cambridge: Cambridge University Press, 1988.

Zammit, T. (1930) *Prehistoric Malta: the Tarxien Temples.* London: H. Milford: Oxford University Press, 1930.

Index

A

Aeolian islands, 16, 27 [note 17], 34 [note 3]
Agnello, Giuseppe 22
Agnello, Santi Luigi 22
Alignments, 5 [note 10]
Allée couverte, 2
Alzoleddha, dolmen 32
Anapo river, 13, 26 [note 7]
Andrian-Werburg (von), Ferdinand 18, 27 [note 21]
Ansaldi, Giuseppe 23
Antoninii Itinerarium, 9
Apulia, 3, 4, 11, 16, 20, 25, 33
Artificial grotto, 13, 14, 18
Assinaro river, 20
Atkinson, Richard 5 [note 11]
Avola dolmen, 20, 21, 22, 25, 33
Axe (in lava material), 18

B

Belgiorno, Francesco Libero 19
Bell-shaped, goblet 32, 34 [notes 2-5]
Belvedere (panoramic area), 25
Bernabò Brea, Luigi 22, 27 [note 14]
Billella, dolmen 31, 32
Boccaletto (small tankard), 11
Borgellusa, contrada 21, 28 [note 34]
Breton, dolmens 1
Bronze age, 3, 11, 13,14, 18, 20, 26 [note 7], 27 [notes 14, 16 & 17], 32, 34 [notes 2-7], 38
Bubbonia, monte 9, 12, 13, 26 [notes 2, 4, 6, 7 & 8], 33
Butera, 11

C

Caltanissetta, 3
Capo Graziano, 16
Cappadocia (ceramic), 27 [note 14]
Carnac, 3, 5 [notes 10 & 23]
Casale, monte 28 [note 27]
Cassibile, 20, 38
Castelluccio, culture 27 [note 14], 28 [note 27], 38
Chamber dolmen, 2, 3, 4, 5 [note 8], 10, 11, 14, 18
Childe, Vere Gordon 1
Ciancio, Salvatore 21, 23
Comiso, 11, 27 [note 15], 38
Corridor tombs, 2, 34 [note 5], 5 [note 6]
Corruggi, 25
Cromlechs, 2, 5 [note 9]

D

Dolmen cysts, 3
Drogheda, 5 [note 8]

E

Elimi, 31
Enchytrismós, 13
Evans, John Davies 6 [notes 18-19], 33

F

False dome, dolmen 2, 5 [note 6], 13, 20
Felci (delle), grotta 37
Femmina morta, site 9
Filicudi (island), 27 [note 17]
Finocchito (site), 38

G

Gaea, the mother goddess 1
Gallery tombs, 2, 3
Gela, 9, 10
Gentili, Vinicio Giorgio 22, 28 [note 33]
Giarratana, 31
Gigantija, 27 [note 16]
Globuled bones, 18
Gozo, 4, 16, 27 [note 16]
Grande, monte 6 [note 14]
Great, cava 18
Griffo, Paolo 22

H

Hagiar Kim, 27[note 16]
Herodotus, 10

I

Iberian, peninsula 16, 32
Iblean, 13, 18, 20
Ireland, 18
Irminio, member 13

K

Kerlescan, 5 [note 10]
Kermario, 5 [note 10]

L

Laghi, Giuseppe 22
Lauro, mount 13
Lazzaro, cava 18, 19, 20, 27 [note 20], 28 [notes 27-30]
Lazzaro, grotta 18, 27 [notes 15 & 26]
Leonardo, member 13
Lerna, 28 [note 27]
Libra, Giuseppe 20
Lipari, 16
Locmariaquer, 27 [note 23]
L'Unica, cava 21
Lùras, 31, 32, 34 [note 6]

M

Maen, 1
Maktorion, 10
Malpasso/Sant'Ippolito, culture 37
Malta, 1, 4, 5, 6[notes 16 & 17], 12, 16, 20, 27 [notes 16, 18 & 19] 28 [note 27], 33, 38
Manéer-Hroec, 27 [note 23]
Manicalunga, castelluccian style 34[note 5]
Masella, grotto 28 [note 27]
Matrensa, style 37
McCall, Daniel F. 22

Megalithic, missionaries 1
Megalithic, temples 4
Megalithism, 32
Melilli, 25
Menéc, 5 [note 10]
Menhirs, 3, 5 [note 10]
Merchants table, 27 [note 23]
Mgiarr, 27 [note 16]
Mnaidra, 27 [note 16]
Modica, Marina di 25
Mont Saint Michel (Le), 5 [note 8]
Mound, 5 [note 8]
Morbihan, 5 [note 8]
Muculufa (La), 6 [note 14]
Mulinello river, 25
Mura Pregne, dolmen 9

N

Neanderthal, 18
Newgrange, 5 [notes 7-8]
Noto, 13, 25, 27 [note 14]

O

Orlandini, Pietro (or Piero) 10
Orsi, Paolo 10, 11
Orthostats, 2
Oval globules, 28 [note 27]

P

Pantalica, culture 11, 13, 26 [note 7], 38
Peloponnese, 28 [note 27]
Petraro, district 25
Piano della fiera, 3, 6 [note 13]
Piano Notaro, culture 37
Piedi Grandi (Big Feet), dolmen 32, 33
Polypode vases, 34 [note 5]

Prince's Tomb, 18, 19
Pseudo dolmen, 20, 25, 33
Pyramids, Egyptian 1

R

Racello, monte 11, 27 [note 15]
Ragusa, 11, 13
Rosolini, 18

S

San Cono, culture 37
San Giacomo, hamlet 13
San Mauro, monte 9
Sante Croci, 28 [note 27]
Sardinia, 3, 11, 16, 20, 32, 34
Sciacca, 9, 11
Sciara, 9
Serraferlicchio, culture 37
Servi (dei), cava 13, 14, 16, 17, 19, 20, 26 [notes 9-11]
Sicanians, 31, 38
Siculo people, 31
Solarino, 24, 25
Sorba, 27 [note 16]
Spain, 1, 5 [note 6], 20, 32, 34, 34 [note 2]
Specchie (small/big) 4
Spongano, 32, 33
Stentinello, culture 37
Stonehenge, 2, 4, 27 [note 23]
Striccoli, Rodolfo 25
Syracuse, 13, 19, 20, 21, 22, 25

T

Tabuto, monte 27 [note 15]
Taol, 1
Tarxien, culture 5, 16, 34
Tellaro river, 13

Tellesimo river 13
Termini Imerese, 9
Thalassaemia (Mediterranean anaemia), 27 [note 13]
Thapsos, culture 38
Tombs, oven 18
Tombs, vault 18
Trilithic, 2, 3, 25
Troy, 28 [note 27]
Tusa, Sebastiano 19

U

Upright stones, 4, 10, 11, 14, 19

V

Villasmundo, 25, 38

Z

Zammit, Themistocles 16
Ziggurats, 1

www.ingramcontent.com/pod-product-compliance
Lightning Source LLC
LaVergne TN
LVHW061253060426
835507LV00017B/2053